Blooming

Grace Finlayson

BookLeaf
Publishing

Presentation by *BookLeaf Publishing*

Web: www.bookleafpub.com

E-mail: info@bookleafpub.com

ISBN: 9789395755122

First edition 2022

DEDICATION

I dedicate this book to everyone and anyone whom I have loved. You all played a role in the creation of this book, of the creation of who I am.

ACKNOWLEDGEMENT

Thank you to anyone who believed I was enough when all I felt was less than.

PREFACE

It's hard realizing that this is for anyone's eyes to
glaze over.
Because every inch of this book is as real
and raw as it gets for me.
These aren't all things I'm proud of, nor things I
feel in this current moment,
but they are a part of this story.
They are all a part of my story.

What now?

I write to heal,
To tend to my garden bed of wounds,
To water the flowers that have been drying out
since the day you left.
I write to feel because it's the only way I've ever
known how.
As I see the words molding together to form a
sentence I realize how I truly felt all along.
But I have written 1000 poems about you,
and all I know is that I'm still broken.
I have thought about my feelings more than I
have ever before.
so much so,
I stopped writing.
I stopped feeling.
I stopped being me.
Because I couldn't bear to string another
sentence together about you.
I couldn't bear to dedicate another piece of my
heart to you.
I have used every trick of the trade to get over
you and yet every single time all I come back to
is wanting you.
-What now?

Right where you needed to go

You will grow.
The seasons will change.
You won't be the same person you once were.
You may not see it right now but one day that
thing that made you change will be the very
thing that led you right where you needed to go.

Our last kiss

I think I'll remember our last kiss more than our
first,
because although the very first felt like I had
finally come home.
The very last felt like someone was hurting my
heart as it happened,
as though I knew the very lips I was touching
were becoming untouchable, becoming a distant
memory.
I tried so hard to not let you go but if this season
of life has taught me anything, it's that if
someone wants to leave you should let them.

Calm before the storm

I knew I loved you more than I had anyone ever
before,
because my heart no longer jumped out of my
chest,
It no longer skipped a beat every time you were
near,
It no longer felt crippled and exhausted after a
long day's work,
it no longer felt like it could never just do its job,
because you made my heart feel at ease.
You helped calm my nervous system in ways
you and I both probably never will fully
understand.
You helped lift me up when I felt as though I had
nothing to hold.
You wrapped my heart up in your arms from the
moment you laid eyes on me,
and you kept it safe as though your life
depended on it.
So why?
Why did you break it?
Why did you work so hard on something, only
to tear it apart?
Were you really protecting me from any less
harm by walking away?

-You told me it was for my own good but all I
see is bad.

Searching

I always liked writing because it was the one
thing I could control.
I could always got to choose whether it was
happy or sad,
thought-provoking or a mere musing.
I got to feel the world at my fingertips,
I got to look at things in ways others didn't,
I got to feel things in ways others couldn't.
All because I was brave enough to try,
all because I knew there was more to this life for
me.
The things I saw growing up most of my peers
didn't,
with these memories engraved in my brain I had
no choice but to keep searching,
to keep searching for more, to keep searching to
feel more,
to keep searching to be more.
-keep searching.

Moments

It's the idea that we as humans are forever
evolving, growing, and changing with every
single moment of our lives.
Because no moment will ever have the
capacity to be the exact same again,
and that's a beautiful thing to know that you
have witnessed so many things for the very first
and last time.
You've been there through it all,
you've been a part of so many beginnings and
endings.
And every moment in between is adding to
every
tiny detail that creates us as we live and breathe.

Learning

I think sometimes I forget that I don't have to
carry every feeling of hurt with me into every
situation.
There will be some that require me to have
learned from my past mistakes but there are also
so many times when I carry all of this pain and
anxiety into situations that don't even warrant
those emotions.
So often I find myself unclenching my jaw and
curled fists because I carry this
anger with me everywhere I go.
But I am learning, I am learning that it is okay to
put down some of your baggage
and not pick it back up again.
I am learning the difference between helpful
fears and crippling anxiety and just how similar
the two can look sometimes.
I am learning that I will always make mistakes
but that learning from them can
sometimes be the biggest blessing in your entire
lifetime.

Hanging on

I'm proud of myself.
This wasn't easy and I thought it would be and
that in itself is a hard pill to swallow.
But I'm doing it, I'm picking my battles,
I am fighting my wars and I know I'll be
so much stronger for it.
-I'm hanging on for myself.

Understanding

It feels like something has changed in me since
we met,
somehow every day that we were together you
taught me how to deal with my problems all
alone,
you taught me to stay quiet and not voice my
concerns,
you taught me how to be composed and lie about
how okay I was.
You taught me how to hide every ounce of
feeling the exact same way you do.
-I finally understand why you are the way you
are.
-I'm so sorry that someone made you this way.

Growing pains

Lately, it's been feeling as if I've outgrown my
own skin,
All of those things that were so scary that I had
to face head-on,
they changed me.
And now it feels like I've grown out of my own
home.
-Is this what growing pains feel like?

Taking back

I'm always second-guessing myself,
refining myself,
slimming down already slim parts of my body
for fear of taking up space.
Society has plagued me with this identity crisis
every day.
Am I enough to rightfully take the space that
someone else could fill?
Am I intelligent enough?
Am I kind enough?
Am I human enough?
But the older I get,
the more people I meet that remind me not
everyone thinks like this.
That not everyone is afraid to take up space the
way I am,
for some fear not taking any at all,
and others will take all the space in the world
just because they can.
So now it is my responsibility now to take back
what is rightfully my space to breathe,
smile,
and exist in.

-You deserve a life filled with endless space
made for you and I'm sorry if you've ever been
made to feel like you couldn't.

Winter

This winter feels darker and drearier than ever
before.
The wind howls louder, the sun abandons us so
early in the afternoons now.
I never knew I loved the summer so much until I
felt the cold of winter.
-I never knew I loved you so much until you
walked away.

Exhausted

I can feel my hipbones sticking out further than
ever before,
my fingers tracing over my bones where jelly
once sat.
Where now lays nothing.
Suddenly I was overwhelmed with remorse for
that part of myself I hadn't gotten to say
goodbye to.
I was always so busy wishing it away,
never stopping to appreciate what I had at the
time.
Never appreciating how it felt to run and walk
with strength,
and how now just getting out of bed now feels
like climbing Mt Everest.
-I got what I wanted but was it ever really worth
it?

Bravery

Being brave doesn't always mean standing up
and being loud and proud,
often it means sitting still,
sitting with it and acting when ready to do so.
Being brave isn't about the insane amounts of
courage that arise in situations of stress,
Real bravery is showing up,
and fighting for the life you want every single
day.

No

No.
I finally muttered under my breath,
No,
I cannot,
will not put up with this internal hatred,
the endless battles all to only feel like I've lost
the war every time I lay my head to
rest.
No.
I finally muttered under my breath to you,
I finally mustered the courage to twist your
words and shove them back in your face.
No,
I don't want you, no I don't love you any longer.
No,
I will never let you ruin another day,
moment,
and especially not this lifetime.
No,
I finally said to myself,
no,
I deserve better than you.
-Learning new meanings to old words.

Stuck

Lately,
I've been detaching myself,
From the people I love,
From the things I love,
From the moving parts of life that I once
yearned for.
I'm stuck with this dull sensation right through
my core.
-Stuck with the constant feeling of never being
satisfied.

Feel it

Give yourself the same amount of time you
would give to someone you love to process the
things that hurt you.
-You are not a machine and it is truly a
wonderful thing that you feel things the way you
do.

Your time

It is your time to shift,
to level up your vibrations,
to harness the parts you love about yourself and
relinquish everything else.
-Your life is awaiting you darling, you just have
to want it bad enough to see it.

Real love

You deserve the kind of love that makes it feel
like the first time.
The kind of love that lifts you up and holds you
above everyone else,
the kind of love that molds you into each other's
lives,
the kind of love that makes your heart pound.
You deserve the kind of love you are dreaming
of.
-Don't settle for anything less.

Balance

Every day I am learning how to perfect the art of
balance.
Every day that I pour from my own cup I know
that I need to replace it,
I know that I need to give grace to the aspects of
life that are gradually growing,
gradually evolving into something tangible,
into something so breathtakingly beautiful.
I am learning how to pour into someone else
without leaving myself empty.
I am learning the power of having space.
I am learning the importance of having a void to
fill.
I am learning how to balance myself in a world
that profits from my inability to.

I'm not the same person.

I don't feel the same way I used to.
The all-consuming, overwhelming anxiety that
fueled my existence.
The crippling depression that pumped through
my veins for so many years.
Although the feeling of falling apart still haunts
me every single day,
because I worked so hard to get here.
I worked so hard to get to a place of not having
my every waking moment consumed by
crippling emotions.
I worked so hard on becoming someone that I'm
proud of.
Because every day that I choose myself I feel a
little bit closer to that person.
-To the person I hope I am and the person I hope
to be.